A Guide to MLA Documentation

with an Appendix on APA Style

Fifth Edition

Joseph F. Trimmer

Ball State University

Houghton Mifflin Company   Boston   New York

As part of Houghton Mifflin's ongoing
commitment to the environment, this text
has been printed on recycled paper.

Senior Sponsoring Editor: Dean Johnson
Senior Project Editor: Janet Young
Production/Design Coordinator: Jennifer Meyer Dare
Senior Manufacturing Coordinator: Marie Barnes
Senior Marketing Manager: Nancy Lyman

Acknowledgments

This guide in part summarizes the documentation style of the Modern Language Association of America as it appears in Joseph Gibaldi, *MLA Handbook for Writers of Research Papers,* 4th ed. (New York: MLA, 1995); and in Joseph Gibaldi, *MLA Style Manual and Guide to Scholarly Publishing,* 2d ed. (New York: MLA, 1998); and on the MLA Web site (http://www.mla.org) published in November 1997. This guide is not a work of the Modern Language Association of America, however, and bears no endorsement from the association. For a fuller presentation of many of the topics covered in this guide, readers should consult the resources listed above.

Printed in the U.S.A.
ISBN: 0-395-938511
Library of Congress Catalog Card Number: 98-72088

123456789-DC-02 01 00 99 98

Contents

1. Preparing the List of Works Cited   1

    Sample Entries: Books   3
    Sample Entries: Articles in Periodicals   7
    Sample Entries: CD-ROMs   9
    Sample Entries: Internet and Web Sources   9
    Sample Entries: Other Sources   12

2. Documenting Sources   14

    Placing and Punctuating the Parenthetical Reference   15
    Citing Sources: Examples   16

3. Using Notes and Parenthetical References   20

4. Implications for Your Research and Composing   21

    Compiling Source Cards   21
    Composing Note Cards   22
    Quoting Sources   22
    Summarizing and Paraphrasing Sources   24
    Avoiding Plagiarism   25

5. Sample Outline and Research Paper   27

6. Abbreviations for MLA Documentation   40

Appendix on APA Style   41

    Preparing the List of References   42
    Sample Entries   43
    Documenting Sources   45

Index   47

This pamphlet explains the style recommended by the Modern Language Association (MLA) for documenting sources in research papers. It also analyzes some of the implications of MLA style for your research and composing. More detailed information is given in the *MLA Handbook* and the *MLA Style Manual*.[1]

MLA style has three major features. First, all sources cited in a paper are listed in a section entitled **Works Cited**, which is located at the end of the paper. Second, material borrowed from another source is documented within the text by a brief parenthetical reference that directs readers to the full citation in the list of works cited. Third, numbered footnotes or endnotes are used to present two types of supplementary information: (1) commentary or explanation that the text cannot accommodate and (2) bibliographical notes that contain several source citations.

1. Preparing the List of Works Cited

In a research paper that follows MLA style, the list of works cited is the *only* place where readers will find complete information about the sources you have cited. For that reason, your list must be thorough and accurate.

The list of works cited appears at the end of your paper and, as its title suggests, *lists only the works you have cited in your paper*. Occasionally, your instructor may ask you to prepare a list of works consulted. That list would include not only the sources you cite but also the sources you consulted as you conducted your research. In either case, MLA prefers Works Cited or Works Consulted to the more limited heading Bibliography (literally, "description of books") because those headings are more likely to accommodate the variety of sources—articles, films, Internet sources—that writers may cite in a research paper.

To prepare the list of works cited, follow these general guidelines:

1. Paginate the Works Cited section as a continuation of your text. If the conclusion of your paper appears on page 8, begin your list on page 9 (unless there is an intervening page of endnotes).

[1] Joseph Gibaldi, *MLA Handbook for Writers of Research Papers*, 4th ed. (New York: MLA, 1995). Joseph Gibaldi, *MLA Style Manual and Guide to Scholarly Publishing*, 2d ed. (New York: MLA, 1998).

2. Double-space between successive lines of an entry and between entries.

3. Begin the first line of an entry flush left, and indent successive lines five spaces or one-half inch.

4. List entries in alphabetical order according to the last name of the author.

5. If you are listing more than one work by the same author, alphabetize the works according to title (excluding the articles *a, an,* and *the*). Instead of repeating the author's name, type *three* hyphens and a period, and then give the title.

6. Underline the titles of works published independently—books, plays, long poems, pamphlets, periodicals, films.

7. Although you do not *need* to underline the spaces between words, a continuous line is easier to type and guarantees that all features of the title are underlined. Type a continuous line under titles unless you are instructed to do otherwise.

8. If you are citing a book whose title includes the title of another book, underline the main title, but do not underline the other title (for example, A Casebook on Ralph Ellison's Invisible Man).

9. Use quotation marks to indicate titles of short works that appear in larger works (for example, ''Minutes of Glory.'' African Short Stories). Also use quotation marks for song titles and for titles of unpublished works, including dissertations, lectures, and speeches.

10. Use arabic numerals except with names of monarchs (Elizabeth II) and except for the preliminary pages of a work (ii–xix), which are traditionally numbered with roman numerals.

11. Use lowercase abbreviations to identify the parts of a work (for example, *vol.* for *volume*), a named translator (*trans.*), and a named editor (*ed.*). However, when these designations follow a period, they should be capitalized (for example, Woolf, Virginia. A Writer's Diary. Ed. Leonard Woolf).

12. Whenever possible, use appropriate shortened forms for the publisher's name (*Random* instead of *Random House*). See the list of abbreviations beginning on page 40.

13. Separate author, title, and publication information with a period followed by *one space.*

14. Use a colon and one space to separate the volume number and year of a periodical from the page numbers (for example, Trimmer, Joseph. ''Memoryscape: Jean Shepherd's Midwest.'' Old Northwest 2 (1976): 357–69).

In addition to these guidelines, MLA recommends procedures for documenting an extensive variety of sources, including electronic sources and nonprint materials such as films and television programs. The following models illustrate sources most commonly cited.

Sample Entries: Books

When citing books, provide the following general categories of information:

Author's last name, first name. Book title. Additional information.

    City of publication: Publishing company, publication date.

Entries illustrating variations on this basic format appear below and are numbered to facilitate reference.

A Book by One Author

1. Boorstin, Daniel J. The Creators: A History of the Heroes of the
   Imagination. New York: Random, 1992.

Two or More Books by the Same Author

2. Garreau, Joel. Edge City: Life on the New Frontier. New York: Doubleday,
   1991.

3. - - -. The Nine Nations of North America. Boston: Houghton, 1981.

A Book by Two or Three Authors

4. Vare, Ethlie Ann, and Greg Ptacek. Mothers of Invention: From the Bra
   to the Bomb: Forgotten Women and Their Unforgettable Ideas. New
   York: Morrow, 1988.

5. Atwan, Robert, Donald McQuade, and John W. Wright. Edsels, Luckies, and
   Frigidaires: Advertising the American Way. New York: Dell, 1979.

A Book by Four or More Authors

6. Belenky, Mary Field, et al. <u>Women's Ways of Knowing: The Development of Self, Voice, and Mind</u>. New York: Basic, 1986.

A Book by a Corporate Author

7. Boston Women's Health Book Collective. <u>Our Bodies, Ourselves: A Book by and for Women</u>. New York: Simon, 1973.

A Book by an Anonymous Author

8. <u>Literary Market Place: The Dictionary of American Book Publishing</u>. 1998 ed. New York: Bowker, 1997.

A Book with an Editor

9. Hall, Donald, ed. <u>The Oxford Book of American Literary Anecdotes</u>. New York: Oxford UP, 1981.

A Book with an Author and an Editor

10. Toomer, Jean. <u>Cane</u>. Ed. Darwin T. Turner. New York: Norton, 1988.

A Book with a Publisher's Imprint

11. Kozol, Jonathan. <u>Illiterate America</u>. New York: Anchor–Doubleday, 1985.

An Anthology or Compilation

12. Valdez, Luis, and Stan Steiner, eds. <u>Aztlan: An Anthology of Mexican American Literature</u>. New York: Vintage–Knopf, 1972.

A Work in an Anthology

13. Silko, Leslie Marmon. ''The Man to Send Rain Clouds.'' <u>Imagining</u>
<u>America: Stories from the Promised Land</u>. Ed. Wesley Brown and
Amy Ling. New York: Persea, 1991. 191–95.

An Introduction, Preface, Foreword, or Afterword

14. Bernstein, Carl. Afterword. <u>Poison Penmanship: The Gentle Art of</u>
<u>Muckraking</u>. By Jessica Mitford. New York: Vintage–Random, 1979.
275–77.

A Multivolume Work

15. Blotner, Joseph. <u>Faulkner: A Biography</u>. 2 vols. New York: Random,
1974.

An Edition Other Than the First

16. Chaucer, Geoffrey. <u>The Riverside Chaucer</u>. Ed. Larry D. Benson. 3rd ed.
Boston: Houghton, 1987.

A Book in a Series

17. McClave, Heather, ed. <u>Women Writers of the Short Story</u>. Twentieth Century
Views. Englewood Cliffs: Spectrum–Prentice, 1980.

A Republished Book

18. Malamud, Bernard. <u>The Natural</u>. 1952. New York: Avon, 1980.

A Signed Article in a Reference Book

19. Tobias, Richard. ''Thurber, James.'' <u>Encyclopedia Americana</u>.
1991 ed.

An Unsigned Article in a Reference Book

20. ''Tharp, Twyla.'' <u>Who's Who of American Women</u>. 17th ed. 1991–92.

A Government Document

21. United States. Cong. House. Committee on the Judiciary. <u>Immigration and</u>
<u>Nationality Act with Amendments and Notes on Related Laws</u>. 7th ed.
Washington: GPO, 1980.

Published Proceedings of a Conference

22. Griggs, John, ed. <u>AIDS: Public Policy Dimensions</u>. Proc. of a conference.
16–17 Jan. 1986. New York: United Hospital Fund of New York,
1987.

A Translation

23. Giroud, Françoise. <u>Marie Curie: A Life</u>. Trans. Lydia Davis. New York:
Holmes, 1986.

A Book with a Title in Its Title

24. Habich, Robert D. <u>Transcendentalism and the</u> Western Messenger:
<u>A History of the Magazine and Its Contributors, 1835–1841</u>.
Rutherford: Fairleigh Dickinson UP, 1985.

A Book Published Before 1900

25. Field, Kate. <u>The History of Bell's Telephone</u>. London, 1878.

An Unpublished Dissertation

26. Geissinger, Shirley Burry. ''Openness versus Secrecy in Adoptive
Parenthood.'' Diss. U of North Carolina at Greensboro, 1984.

A Published Dissertation

27. Ames, Barbara Edwards. <u>Dreams and Painting: A Case Study of the</u>
<u>Relationship between an Artist's Dreams and Painting</u>. Diss. U of
Virginia, 1978. Ann Arbor: UMI, 1979. 7928021.

Sample Entries: Articles in Periodicals

When citing articles in periodicals, provide the following general categories
of information:

Author's last name, first name. ''Article title.'' <u>Periodical title</u> Date: inclusive
pages.

Entries illustrating variations on this basic format appear below and are
numbered to facilitate reference.

A Signed Article from a Daily Newspaper

28. Barringer, Felicity. ''Where Many Elderly Live, Signs of the Future.'' <u>New</u>
<u>York Times</u> 7 Mar. 1993, nat. ed., sec. 1: 12.

An Unsigned Article from a Daily Newspaper

29. ''Infant Mortality Down; Race Disparity Widens.'' <u>Washington Post</u> 12 Mar.
1993: A12.

An Article from a Monthly or Bimonthly Magazine

30. Wills, Garry. ''The Words That Remade America: Lincoln at Gettysburg.''
<u>Atlantic</u> June 1992: 57–79.

An Article from a Weekly or Biweekly Magazine

31. Trillin, Calvin. ''Culture Shopping.'' <u>New Yorker</u> 15 Feb. 1993:
48–51.

An Article in a Journal with Continuous Pagination

32. Elbow, Peter. ''Ranking, Evaluating, and Linking: Sorting Out Three Forms of Judgment.'' College English 55 (1993): 187–206.

An Article in a Journal That Numbers Pages in Each Issue Separately

33. Seely, Bruce. ''The Saga of American Infrastructure: A Republic Bound Together.'' Wilson Quarterly 17.1 (1993): 19–39.

An Editorial

34. ''A Question of Medical Sight.'' Editorial. Plain Dealer [Cleveland, OH] 11 Mar. 1993: 6B.

A Review

35. Morson, Gary Soul. ''Coping with Utopia.'' Rev. of Soviet Civilization: A Cultural History, by Andrei Sinyavsky. American Scholar 61 (1992): 132–38.

An Article Whose Title Contains a Quotation or a Title Within Quotation Marks

36. DeCuir, Andre L. ''Italy, England and the Female Artist in George Eliot's 'Mr. Gilfil's Love–Story.' '' Studies in Short Fiction 29 (1992): 67–75.

An Abstract from *Dissertation Abstracts* or *Dissertation Abstracts International*

37. Creek, Mardena Bridges. ''Myth, Wound, Accommodation: American Literary Responses to the War in Vietnam.'' DAI 43 (1982): 3539A. Ball State U.

Sample Entries: CD-ROMs

When citing information from CD-ROMs, provide the following general categories of information:

Author's last name, first name. ''Article title of printed source or printed

analogue.'' Periodical title of printed source or printed analogue Date:

inclusive pages. Title of database. CD-ROM. Name of vendor or computer

service. Electronic publication date or date of access.

Entries illustrating variations on this basic format appear below and are numbered to facilitate reference.

CD-ROM: Periodical Publication with Printed Source or Printed Analogue

38. West, Cornel. ''The Dilemma of the Black Intellectual.'' Critical Quarterly

29 (1987): 39–52. MLA International Bibliography. CD-ROM. Silver

Platter. Feb. 1995.

CD-ROM: Nonperiodical Publication

39. Cinemania 97. CD-ROM. Redmond: Microsoft, 1996.

CD-ROM: A Work in More Than One Electronic Medium

40. Mozart. CD-ROM. Laser disk. Union City, CA: Ebook, 1992.

Sample Entries: Internet and Web Sources

When citing information from Internet and World Wide Web sources, pro-vide the following general categories of information:

Author's last name, first name. ''Article title'' or Book title. Publication

information for any printed version. Or subject line of forum or discussion

group. Indication of online posting or home page. Title of electronic journal.

Date of electronic publication. Page numbers or the numbers of paragraphs or sections. Name of institution or organization sponsoring Web site. Date of access to the source <electronic address or URL>.

The speed of change in the electronic world means that particular features for citing Internet and Web sources are constantly evolving. The best way to confirm the accuracy of your citations is to check the MLA Web site (<http://www.mla.org>).

Entries illustrating variations on the basic format appear below and are numbered to facilitate reference.

A Professional Site

41. <u>MLA on the Web</u>. 25 November 1997. Modern Language Association of America. 25 Mar. 1998 <http://www.mla.org>.

A Personal Site

42. Hawisher, Gail. Home page. University of Illinois Urbana-Champaign/The Women, Information Technology, and Scholarship Colloquium. 18 Mar. 1998 <http://www.art.uiuc.edu/wits/members/hawisher.html>.

A Book

43. Conrad, Joseph. Lord Jim. London: Blackwoods, 1900. <u>Oxford Text Archive</u>. 12 July 1993. Oxford University Computing Services. 20 Feb. 1998 <ftp://ota.ox.ac.uk/pub/ota/public/english/conrad/lordjim.1824>.

A Poem

44. Hampl, Patricia. ''Who We Will Love.'' <u>Woman Before an Aquarium.</u> Pittsburgh: U of Pittsburgh P, 1978: 27–28. A Poem a Week. Rice University. 13 Mar. 1998 <http://www.ruf.rice.edu/~alisa/Jun24html>.

An Article in a Reference Database

45. ''Women in American History.'' <u>Britannica Online</u> Vers. 98.1.1. Nov. 1997.

     Encyclopedia Britannica. 10 Mar. 1998

     <http://www.britannica.com>.

An Article in a Journal

46. Bieder, Robert A. ''The Representation of Indian Bodies in Nineteenth-

     Century American Anthropology.'' <u>The American Indian Quarterly</u>

     20.2 (1996). 28 Mar. 1998

     <http://www/uoknor.edu/aiq/aiq202.html#beider>.

An Article in a Magazine

47. Levine, Judith. ''I Surf, Therefore I Am.'' <u>Salon</u> 29 July 1997. 9 Dec. 1997

     <http://www.salonmagazine.com/July97/mothers/surfing.970729.html>.

A Review

48. Roth, Martha. ''A Tantalizing Remoteness.'' Rev. of <u>Jane Austen: A</u>

     <u>Biography</u> by Claire Tomalin. <u>Hungry Mind Review</u> Winter 1997.

     10 Mar. 1998

     <http://www.bookwire.com/HMR/nonfiction/read.review$5376>.

A Posting to a Discussion Group

49. Inman, James. ''Re: Technologist.'' Online posting. 24 Sept. 1997. Alliance

     for Computers in Writing. 27 Mar. 1998

     <acw-l@unicorn.acs.ttu.edu>

A Personal E-mail Message

50. Penning, Sarah. ''Mentor Advice.'' E-mail to Rai Peterson. 6 May 1995.

Sample Entries: Other Sources

Films; Radio and Television Programs

51. <u>The Last Emperor</u>. Dir. Bernardo Bertolucci. With John Lone and Peter
O'Toole. Columbia, 1987.

52. ''If God Ever Listened: A Portrait of Alice Walker.'' <u>Horizons</u>. Prod. Jane
Rosenthal. NPR. WBST, Muncie. 3 Mar. 1984.

53. ''The Hero's Adventure.'' <u>Moyers: Joseph Campbell and the Power of Myth</u>.
Prod. Catherine Tatge. PBS. WNET, New York. 23 May 1988.

Performances

54. <u>A Walk in the Woods</u>. By Lee Blessing. Dir. Des McAnuff. With Sam
Waterston and Robert Prosky. Booth Theatre, New York. 17 May
1988.

55. Ozawa, Seiji, cond. Boston Symphony Orch. Concert. Symphony Hall, Boston.
30 Sept. 1988.

Recordings

56. Mozart, Wolfgang A. <u>Cosi Fan Tutte</u>. Record. With Kiri Te Kanawa,
Frederica von Stade, David Rendall, and Philippe Huttenlocher. Cond.
Alain Lombard. Strasbourg Philharmonic Orch. RCA, SRL3–2629, 1978.

57. Simon, Paul. ''Under African Skies.'' <u>Graceland</u>. Audiotape. Warner,
4–25447, 1986.

Works of Art

58. Botticelli, Sandro. <u>Giuliano de' Medici</u>. Samuel H. Kress Collection. National
Gallery of Art, Washington.

59. Rodin, Auguste. <u>The Gate of Hell</u>. Rodin Museum, Paris.

Maps and Charts

60. <u>Sonoma and Napa Counties</u>. Map. San Francisco: California State Automobile Assn., 1984.

Cartoons and Advertisements

61. Addams, Charles. Cartoon. <u>New Yorker</u> 22 Feb. 1988: 33.

62. Air France. ''The Fine Art of Flying.'' Advertisement. <u>Travel and Leisure</u> May 1988: 9.

Published and Unpublished Letters

63. Fitzgerald, F. Scott. ''To Ernest Hemingway.'' 1 June 1934. <u>The Letters of F. Scott Fitzgerald</u>. Ed. Andrew Turnbull. New York: Scribner's, 1963. 308–10.

64. Stowe, Harriet Beecher. Letter to George Eliot. 25 May 1869. Berg Collection. New York: New York Public Library.

Interviews

65. Ellison, Ralph. ''Indivisible Man.'' Interview. By James Alan McPherson. <u>Atlantic</u> Dec. 1970: 45–60.

66. Diamond, Carol. Telephone interview. 27 Dec. 1988.

Lectures, Speeches, and Addresses

67. Russo, Michael. ''A Painter Speaks His Mind.'' Museum of Fine Arts. Boston, 5 Aug. 1984.

68. Baker, Houston A., Jr. ''The Presidential Address.'' MLA Convention. New York, 28 Dec. 1992.

2. Documenting Sources

The purpose of a parenthetical reference is to document a source briefly, clearly, and accurately. Brevity can be accomplished in three ways.

1.   Cite the author's last name and the page number(s) of the source in parentheses.

One historian argues that since the invention of television ''our politics, religion, news, athletics, education and commerce have been transformed into congenial adjuncts of show business, largely without protest or even much popular notice'' (Postman 3–4).

2.   Use the author's last name in your sentence, and place only the page number(s) of the source in parentheses.

Postman points out that since the invention of television ''our politics, religion, news, athletics, education and commerce have been transformed into congenial adjuncts of show business, largely without protest or even much popular notice'' (3–4).

3.   Give the author's last name in your sentence when you are citing the *entire* work rather than a *specific* section or passage, and omit any parenthetical reference.

Postman argues that television has changed virtually every aspect of our culture into a form of show business.

Each of those in-text references is brief and clear and refers readers to a specific and complete citation listed in Works Cited. The citation looks like this:

Works Cited

Postman, Neil. Amusing Ourselves to Death: Public Discourse in the Age of Show

Business. New York: Penguin–Viking, 1985.

Placing and Punctuating the Parenthetical Reference

To avoid clutter in sentences, MLA recommends placing the parenthetical reference at the end of the sentence but before the final period. Notice that there is no punctuation mark between the author's name and the page citation.

In the nineteenth century, the supposed golden age of American education, ''college faculties acted as disciplinary tribunals, periodically reviewing violations of rules . . .'' (Graff 25).

On some occasions, you may want to place the reference *within* your sentence to clarify its relationship to the part of the sentence it documents. In such instances, place the reference at the end of the clause but before the necessary comma.

Graff suggests that even though college faculties in the nineteenth century ''acted as disciplinary tribunals, periodically reviewing violations of rules'' (25), the myth persists that they taught in the golden age of American education.

When the reference documents a long quotation that is set off from the text, place it at the end of the passage but *after* the final period.

Gerald Graff's description of the college in the nineteenth century corrects the popular myth about the golden age of American education:

College faculties acted as disciplinary tribunals, periodically reviewing violations of rules such as those requiring students to attend chapel services early every morning, to remain in their rooms for hours every day, and to avoid the snares of town. Nor were these restrictions relaxed for the many students in their late twenties or older, who lived alongside freshmen as young as fourteen. The classes themselves, conducted by the system of daily recitations, were said to have ''the fearsome atmosphere of a police-station.'' (25)

Works Cited

Graff, Gerald. <u>Professing Literature: An Institutional History</u>. Chicago: U of

    Chicago P, 1987.

Citing Sources: Examples

Frequently, you will need to cite sources that are not as straightforward as the examples given above. In those cases, you will need to modify the standard format according to the variations illustrated below. Each example is followed by the appropriate entry that would appear in the list of works cited.

1. Citing one work by the author of two or more works

If your list of works cited contains two or more titles by the same author, place a comma after the author's last name, add a shortened version of the title of the work, and then supply the relevant page numbers. Another solution is to cite the author's last name and title in your sentence and then add the page numbers in a parenthetical reference.

Once society reaches a certain stage of industrial growth, it will shift its

energies to the production of services (Toffler, <u>Future</u> 221).

Toffler argues in <u>The Third Wave</u> that society has gone through two eras

(agricultural and industrial) and is now entering another – the information

age (26).

Works Cited

Toffler, Alvin. <u>Future Shock</u>. New York: Random, 1970.

– – –. <u>The Third Wave</u>. New York: Morrow, 1980.

2. Citing one work by an author who has the same last name as another author in your list of works cited

When your list contains sources by two or more authors with the same last name, avoid confusion by adding the initial of the author's first name in the parenthetical reference and the author's first name in your sentence. In the list of works cited, the two authors should be alphabetized according to first name.

Critics have often debated the usefulness of the psychological approach to literary interpretation (F. Hoffman 317).

Daniel Hoffman argues that folklore and myth provide valuable insights for the literary critic (9–15).

Works Cited

Hoffman, Daniel G. Form and Fable in American Fiction. New York: Oxford UP, 1961.

Hoffman, Frederick J. Freudianism and the Literary Mind. Baton Rouge: Louisiana State UP, 1945.

3. Citing a multivolume work

If you are citing one volume from a multivolume work, indicate in your parenthetical reference the specific volume you used.

William Faulkner's initial reluctance to travel to Stockholm to receive the Nobel Prize produced considerable consternation in the American embassy (Blotner 2: 1347).

Works Cited

Blotner, Joseph. Faulkner: A Biography. 2 vols. New York: Random, 1974.

4. Citing a work by more than one author

If you are citing a book by two or three authors, you may supply their last names in a parenthetical reference or in your sentence. To sustain the readability of your sentence if you are citing a book by four or more authors, use the first author's last name and *et al.* ("and others") in a parenthetical reference or in your sentence.

Boller and Story interpret the Declaration of Independence as Thomas Jefferson's attempt to list America's grievances against England (2: 62).

Other historians view the Declaration of Independence as Jefferson's attempt to formulate the principles of America's political philosophy (Norton et al. 141).

Works Cited

Boller, Paul F., Jr., and Ronald Story. <u>A More Perfect Union: Documents in U.S.</u>

<u>History</u>. 2 vols. 3rd ed. Boston: Houghton, 1992.

Norton, Mary Beth, et al. <u>A People and a Nation: A History of the United States</u>.

4th ed. Boston: Houghton, 1994.

5. Citing a work by title

In the list of works cited, alphabetize works by anonymous authors according to the first main word in the title. The initial articles *a, an,* and *the* are not counted as first words. A shortened version of the title—or the title itself, if it is short—replaces the author's last name in the text citation or parenthetical reference. If you shorten the title, be sure to begin with the word by which the source is alphabetized in the list of works cited.

The recent exhibit of nineteenth-century patent models at the

Cooper-Hewitt Museum featured plans for such inventions as the Rotating

Blast-Producing Chair, an Improved Creeping-Doll, and the Life-Preserving

Coffin: In Doubtful Cases of Actual Death (''Talk'').

Notice that this example follows MLA's recommendation to omit page numbers in a parenthetical reference when citing a one-page article.

Works Cited

''The Talk of the Town.'' <u>New Yorker</u> 16 July 1984: 23.

6. Citing a work by a corporate author or government agency

If the author of your source is a corporation or a government agency, you may include the appropriate citation within parentheses (American Telephone and Telegraph 3). It is more graceful, however, to include this information in your sentence, particularly if you are citing several corporate or government reports in one text.

American Telephone and Telegraph's <u>Annual Report</u> for 1982 announced

that the corporation had reached a turning point in its history (3).

Works Cited

American Telephone and Telegraph. <u>Annual Report 1982</u>. New York: American

    Telephone and Telegraph, 1983.

7. Citing literary works

Because literary works—novels, plays, poems—are available in many editions, MLA recommends that you provide information in addition to page numbers, so that readers using editions different from yours can locate the passage you are citing. After the page number, add a semicolon and other appropriate information, using lowercase abbreviations such as *pt., sec., ch.*

Although Flaubert sees Madame Bovary for what she is- -a silly, romantic

woman- -he insists that ''none of us can ever express the exact measure of

his needs or his thoughts or his sorrows'' and that all of us ''long to make

music that will melt the stars'' (216; pt. 2, ch. 12).

Works Cited

Flaubert, Gustave. <u>Madame Bovary: Patterns of Provincial Life</u>. Trans. Francis

    Steegmuller. New York: Modern Library–Random, 1957.

When citing classic verse plays and poems, omit all page numbers and document by division(s) and line(s), using periods to separate the various numbers. You can also use appropriate abbreviations to designate certain well-known works. For example, *Od.* 8.326 refers to book 8, line 326, of Homer's *Odyssey*. Do not use the abbreviation *l.* or *ll.* to indicate lines because the letters can be confused with numbers.

Also, as shown in the *Odyssey* citation given above, use arabic numerals rather than roman numerals to indicate divisions and page numbers. Some teachers still prefer to use roman numerals for documenting acts and scenes in plays (for example, *Macbeth* III.iv). If your instructor does not insist on this practice, follow MLA style and use arabic numerals (and appropriate abbreviations) to cite famous plays—*Mac.* 3.4.

8. Citing more than one work in a single parenthetical reference

If you need to include two or more works in a single parenthetical reference, document each reference according to the normal pattern, but separate each citation with a semicolon.

(Oleson 59; Trimble 85; Hylton 63)

Works Cited

Hylton, Marion Willard. ''On a Trail of Pollen: Momaday's House Made of

Dawn.'' Critique: Studies in Modern Fiction 14.2 (1972): 60–69.

Oleson, Carole. ''The Remembered Earth: Momaday's House Made of Dawn.''

South Dakota Review 11 (1973): 59–78.

Trimble, Martha Scott. N. Scott Momaday. Boise State College Western Writers

Series. Boise: Boise State Col., 1973.

Although MLA style provides this procedure for documenting multiple citations within a parenthetical reference, MLA recommends citing multiple sources in a numbered bibliographic note rather than parenthetically in the text.

3. Using Notes and Parenthetical References

In MLA style, notes (preferably endnotes) are reserved for two specific purposes.

1. **To supply additional commentary on the information in the text**

    Thurber's reputation continued to grow until the 1950s, when he was forced to give up drawing because of his blindness.[1]

Note

[1] Thurber's older brother accidentally shot him in the eye with an arrow when they were children, causing the immediate loss of that eye. He gradually lost the sight of the other eye because of complications from the accident and a cataract.

2. **To list (and perhaps evaluate) several sources or to refer readers to additional sources**

    The argument that American policy in Vietnam was on the whole morally justified has come under attack from many quarters.[1]

Note

[1] For a useful sampling of opinion, see Draper 32 and Nardin and Slater 437.

Notice that the sources cited in this note are documented like parenthetical references and the note itself directs readers to the complete citation in the list of works cited.

Works Cited

Draper, Theodore. ''Ghosts of Vietnam.'' <u>Dissent</u> 26 (1979): 30–41.

Nardin, Terry, and Jerome Slater. ''Vietnam Revisited.'' <u>World Politics</u> 33

(1981): 436–48.

As illustrated above, a note is signaled with a superscript numeral (a numeral raised above the line) typed at an appropriate place in the text (most often at the end of a sentence). The note itself, identified by a matching number followed by a space, appears at the end of the text (an endnote) or at the bottom of the page (a footnote). MLA recommends that you keep such notes to a minimum so that readers are not distracted from your main point.

4. Implications for Your Research and Composing

MLA style emphasizes the importance of following the procedures for planning and writing the research paper outlined in any standard writing textbook. In particular, MLA style requires you to devote considerable attention to certain steps in your research and composing.

Compiling Source Cards

Once you have located sources that you suspect will prove useful, fill out a source card on each item. List the source in the appropriate format (use the formats shown in the guidelines for preparing the list of works cited, pages 1–13). To guarantee that each card is complete and accurate, take your information directly from the source rather than from a card catalog or a bibliographical index. Your collection of cards will help you keep track of your sources throughout your research. Alphabetizing the cards will enable you to prepare a provisional list of works cited.

The provisional list must be in place *before* you begin writing your paper. You may expand or refine the list as you write, but to document each source in your text, you first need to know its correct citation. Thus, although Works Cited will be the last section of your paper, you must prepare it first.

Composing Note Cards

Note taking demands that you read, select, interpret, and evaluate the information that will form the substance of your paper. After you return books and articles to the library, your notes will be the only record of your research. If you have taken notes carelessly, you will be in trouble when you try to use them in the body of your paper. Many students inadvertently plagiarize because they are working from inaccurate note cards. As you select information from a source, use one of three methods to record it on an individual note card: quoting, summarizing, or paraphrasing.

Quoting Sources

Although quoting an author's text word for word is the easiest way to record information, use this method selectively and quote only the passages that deal directly with your subject in memorable language. When you copy a quotation onto a note card, place quotation marks at the beginning and the end of the passage. If you decide to omit part of the passage, use ellipsis points to indicate that you have omitted words from the original source. To indicate an omission from the middle of a sentence, use three periods (. . .), and leave a space before and after each period. For an omission at the end of a sentence, use three spaced periods following the sentence period.

To move a quotation from a note card to your paper, making it fit smoothly into the flow of your text, use one of the following methods.

1. **Work the quoted passage into the syntax of your sentence.**

Morrison points out that social context prevented the authors of slave narratives ''from dwelling too long or too carefully on the more sordid details of their experience'' (109).

2. **Introduce the quoted passage with a sentence and a colon.**

Commentators have tried to account for the decorum of most slave narratives by discussing social context: ''popular taste discouraged the writers from dwelling too long or too carefully on the more sordid details of their experience'' (Morrison 109).

3. **Set off the quoted passage with an introductory sentence followed by a colon.**

This method is reserved for long quotations (four or more lines of prose; three or more lines of poetry). Double-space the quotation, and indent it ten spaces or one inch from the left margin. Because this special placement identifies the passage as a quotation, do not enclose it within quotation marks. Notice that the final period goes *before* rather than *after* the parenthetical reference. Leave one space after the final period.

Toni Morrison, in ''The Site of Memory,'' explains how social context shaped slave narratives:

> . . . no slave society in the history of the world wrote more— —or more thoughtfully— —about its own enslavement. The milieu, however, dictated the purpose and the style. The narratives are instructive, moral and obviously representative. Some of them are patterned after the sentimental novel that was in vogue at the time. But whatever the level of eloquence or the form, popular taste discouraged the writers

from dwelling too long or too carefully on the more sordid details of their experience. (109)

Summarizing and Paraphrasing Sources

Summarizing and paraphrasing an author's text are the most efficient ways to record information. The terms *summary* and *paraphrase* are often used interchangeably to describe a brief restatement of the author's ideas in your own words, but they may be used more precisely to designate different procedures. A *summary* condenses the content of a lengthy passage. When you write a summary, you reformulate the main idea and outline the main points that support it. A *paraphrase* restates the content of a short passage. When you write a paraphrase, you reconstruct the passage phrase by phrase, recasting the author's words in your own.

A summary or a paraphrase is intended as a complete and objective presentation of an author's ideas, so do not distort the original passage by omitting major points or by adding your own opinion. Because the words of a summary or a paraphrase are yours, they are not enclosed by quotation marks. But because the ideas you are restating came from someone else, you need to cite the source on your note card and in your text. (See "Avoiding Plagiarism," page 25.)

The following examples illustrate two common methods of introducing a summary or a paraphrase into your paper.

1. **Summary of a long quotation (see the Morrison quotation on page 23)**

Often, the best way to proceed is to name the author of a source in the body of your sentence and place the page numbers in parentheses. This procedure informs your reader that you are about to quote or paraphrase. It also gives you an opportunity to state the credentials of the authority you are citing.

Award-winning novelist Toni Morrison argues that although slaves wrote many powerful narratives, the context of their enslavement prevented them from telling the whole truth about their lives (109).

2. **Paraphrase of a short quotation (see the fourth sentence of the Morrison quotation on page 23)**

You may decide to vary the pattern of documentation by presenting the information from a source and placing the author's name and page numbers in parentheses at the end of the sentence. This method is particularly useful if you have already established the identity of your source in a previous sentence and now want to develop the author's ideas in some detail without having to clutter your sentences with constant references to his or her name.

Slave narratives sometimes imitated the popular fiction of their era

(Morrison 109).

Works Cited

Morrison, Toni. ''The Site of Memory.'' <u>Inventing the Truth: The Art and Craft</u>

   <u>of Memoir</u>. Ed. William Zinsser. Boston: Houghton, 1987. 101–24.

Avoiding Plagiarism

Plagiarism is using someone else's words or ideas without giving proper credit—or without giving any credit at all—to the writer of the original. Whether plagiarism is intentional or unintentional, it is a serious offense that you can avoid by adhering to the advice for research and composing outlined above.

The following excerpt is from Robert Hughes's *The Fatal Shore,* an account of the founding of Australia. The examples of how students tried to use this excerpt illustrate the problem of plagiarism.

Original Version

Transportation did not stop crime in England or even slow it down. The ''criminal class'' was not eliminated by transportation, and could not be, because transportation did not deal with the causes of crime.

Version A

Transportation did not stop crime in England or even slow it down. Criminals were not eliminated by transportation because transportation did not deal with the causes of crime.

Version A is plagiarism. Because the writer of Version A does not indicate in the text or in a parenthetical reference that the words and ideas belong to Hughes, her readers will believe the words are hers. She has stolen the words and ideas and has attempted to cover the theft by changing or omitting an occasional word.

Version B

Robert Hughes points out that transportation did not stop crime in England or even slow it down. The criminal class was not eliminated by transportation, and could not be, because transportation did not deal with the causes of crime (168).

Version B is also plagiarism, even though the writer acknowledges his source and documents the passage with a parenthetical reference. He has worked from careless notes and has misunderstood the difference between quoting and paraphrasing. He has copied the original word for word yet has supplied no quotation marks to indicate the extent of the borrowing. As written and documented, the passage masquerades as a paraphrase when in fact it is a direct quotation.

Version C

Hughes argues that transporting criminals from England to Australia ''did not stop crime. . . . The 'criminal class' was not eliminated by transportation, and could not be, because transportation did not deal with the causes of crime'' (168).

Version C is one satisfactory way of handling this source material. The writer has identified her source at the beginning of the sentence, letting readers know who is being quoted. She then explains the concept of transportation in her own words, placing within quotation marks the parts of the original she wants to quote and using ellipsis points to delete the parts she wants to omit. She provides a parenthetical reference to the page number in the source listed in Works Cited.

Works Cited

Hughes, Robert. The Fatal Shore. New York: Knopf, 1987.

5. Sample Outline and Research Paper

The author of the following research paper used many features of MLA style to document her paper. At her instructor's request, she first submitted a final version of her thesis and outline. Adhering to MLA style, she did not include a title page with her outline or her paper. Instead, she typed her name, her instructor's name, the course title, and the date on separate lines (double-spacing between lines) at the upper left margin. Then, after double-spacing again, she typed the title of her paper, double-spaced, and started the first line of her text. On page 1 and successive pages, she typed her last name and the page number in the upper right-hand corner, as recommended by MLA.

Gwen Vickery

Mr. Johnson

English 104

21 November 1996

 Is Anybody Out There?: The Value of Chat Groups on the Internet

Thesis: Meaningful conversations {in chat groups} are possible, but

finding them might take time.

I. Chat groups have created a cultural controversy.

    A. They provide real support for some people.

    B. They also exclude many people.

II. Chat groups have serious limitations.

    A. People talk only to people like them.

    B. Poor people have no access to these conversations.

III. The quality of conversation in chat groups is inconsistent.

    A. Too many charlatans and too few civic leaders participate
        in chat groups.

    B. Too many virtual conversations are simply junk
        conversations.

IV. Despite their problems, chat groups have many supporters.

    A. Some need the companionship of conversations.

    B. Some like the freedom of textual identity.

    C. Some look for self-affirmation in textual conversations.

V. Chat groups are here to stay.

    A. Some are good; some are bad.

    B. Individuals will have to decide how much time and money
        to invest in searching for meaningful conversations.

1/2"

Vickery 1

1"

Gwen Vickery

English 104

Mr. Johnson

21 November 1996

Is Anybody Out There?: The Value of Chat Groups

on the Internet

In the modern world, where friendly mom-and-pop stores, cozy bars, PTA meetings, and pot-luck dinners are being replaced by online bank tellers, drive-thru liquor stores, televised classrooms, and fast-food chains, more and more people are feeling alienated and isolated. They yearn for friends, for interaction, for communities. Since these needs cannot be met down the street, people are looking down the line (online, that is). The chat rooms (MUDs and MOOs) on the Internet provide a place for people to meet, express themselves, find support, or pass the time by engaging in friendly conversation. The possibilities for communication are endless, but this optimism for ''what could be'' should be tempered by a look at ''what is.'' People exploring the chat rooms for intellectual stimulation and interesting discussions are likely to be disappointed. This virtual reality has yet to filter out the banality, stupidity, bigotry, and chauvinism that are all too common in the real world. If the explorer perseveres, however, he or she may find a few

Double-space

Indent five spaces

1"

Vickery 2

Masterpiece Theatres amid the thousands of Beavis and Butt-
heads. Meaningful conversations are possible, but finding them
might take time.

When John Perry Barlow's fiancé died of a heart attack, he
was overcome with grief and despair. Since he had been living in
New York with his future wife, his family and friends back home
had never met her. Needing to talk, but feeling awkward, he
turned to the Internet. He was touched by the responses he
received:

Long quotation: A quotation of more than four lines is set off from text and is *not* placed in quotation marks.

> They told me of their own tragedies and what they had
> done to survive them. As humans have done since
> words were first uttered, we shared the second most
> common human experience, death, with an
> openheartedness that would have caused grave
> uneasiness in physical America, where the whole topic
> is so cloaked in denial as to be considered obscene. (56)

But although Barlow's experience was positive, he still has
reservations about the Internet, especially about the kinds of people
he meets. He feels that ''women, children, old people, poor people, and
the genuinely blind'' are conspicuously absent, as are ''the illiterate
and the continent of Africa'' (54). Since he had been led to believe
that cyberspace was teeming with human diversity, he was
disillusioned. He concludes that cyberspace is inhabited by ''white
males under 50 with plenty of computer-terminal time, great typing
skills, high math SATs, [and] strongly held opinions on just about

Vickery 3

everything'' (55). Barlow still uses the Net, but his enthusiasm has

cooled.

M. Kadi would agree with Barlow that the Internet, hailed as

the great social leveler, is really just as discriminatory as real life:

Short quotation: The quotation is introduced with an independent clause and set off by a colon.

''What this whole delirious, interconnected, global community of a

world needs is a little reality check'' (57). The cost of subscribing

to an online community such as America Online, Kadi says, is

conservatively estimated at twenty dollars or less per month.

People from the lower economic classes cannot afford such a

luxury. And even if they could afford to join, would anybody hear

their stories or learn from their experiences? Kadi doesn't think so.

Since the Internet provides an overwhelming selection of topics

to choose from, most people are going to limit themselves to those

discussions that speak to their immediate concerns:

> So J. is going to ignore all the support groups——after
> all, J. is a normal, well-adjusted person, and all of J.'s
> friends are normal, well-adjusted people; what does
> J. need to know about alcoholism or incest victims? J.
> Individual is white. So J. Individual is going to ignore all
> the multicultural folders. J. couldn't give a hoot about
> gender issues and does not want to discuss religion or
> philosophy. Ultimately, J. Individual does not engage in
> topics that do not interest J. Individual. So who is J.
> meeting? Why, people who are just like J. (Kadi 59)

When ideas are being discussed that challenge an individual's

belief systems, values, and opinions, does the average person really

Vickery 4

stop and listen with an open mind, provide alternative viewpoints, and work toward a mutual consensus, or does he/she fight back with insults or simply leave the room?

More and more people are becoming disillusioned with the promise of Internet diversity, and as they realize that the Internet's demographics mimic real life, their optimism for a truly democratic online society fades. Bill Machrone notes, ''The Web is not doing a particularly good job of reaching out to the poor and disadvantaged'', and he concludes, ''The idea of a new democracy based on electronic pluralism is so far from reality that it's laughable'' (83). Stacy Horn, dismayed by ''the Internet's testosterone-heavy demographics,'' decided to provide private accounts for women (qtd. in Elmer-Dewitt 56). According to Philip Elmer-Dewitt, this trend may continue as people ''withdraw within their walled communities and never venture again into the Internet's public spaces'' (56). Some universities have determined the MUDs are a ''frivolous use of computer systems'' and have prohibited their use as a ''recreational activity that wastes system resources'' (Masinter 1).

Democracy on the Internet is an ideal, a myth, a pipe dream, and a misrepresentation of reality according to several critics. Not only is Internet access reserved for the economically stable, not only are huge portions of our population not represented, but the quality of most of the Internet discussions is in a sad state.

Short quotation: Author is identified at the beginning of the sentence and quotation is worked into the sentence.

Vickery 5

Although Evan Schwartz sees the positive potential of the
Internet to serve as a surrogate community, he does not think
that a true ''democracy'' can exist on the Net, at least not at this
time:

> Internet enthusiasts sometimes see virtual community
> as a panacea for all sorts of social ills. They go a bit far,
> for example, when they hold out the possibility that the
> Internet could become a forum for electronic democracy.
> The people conversing on the Internet and other online
> services are, by and large, not a bunch of civic leaders.
> The untamed, free-wheeling nature of cyberspace means
> that it is often filled with every skinhead, Trekkie,
> religious zealot, and Limbaugh-wannabe with a new
> theory on how the world should work. The Internet is
> not—at least not now—a town hall meeting. (40)

Paraphrase: Author is identified at the beginning of the sentence in which he is paraphrased.

Gary Chapman would agree with this statement. He is fascinated
by the Internet because it has become a locale where the rude, crude,
and socially unacceptable can unabashedly attack those who are
trying to have a genuine conversation. Chapman believes there are
''millions of electronic Walter Mittys'' whose only purpose is to
relieve their own aggressions and fantasies (14). But even if these
pests were eliminated, Chapman's assessment would not improve:

> Even without all the cranks, poseurs, charlatans,
> fetishists, single-issue monomaniacs, sex-starved lonely
> hearts, mischievous teenagers, sexists, racists and right-

Vickery 6

wing haranguers, many participants in unstructured

Internet conversations have little of interest to say but a

lot of room in which to say it. (14)

   If, by some chance, you find a reasonable, interesting person to

talk to, you can be assured that your conversation will be

''discovered by someone with a hobby horse or an abrasive

personality or both, and there are few reliable ways to shunt such

people elsewhere'' (Chapman 14–15). The prognosis is bad, but

despite the mediocrity and the pesky intruders, people are still

seduced by the Internet's promise of community.

   People are still meeting, still discussing, still flirting (or worse)

despite the hazards. Is this good or bad? Rajiv Rao approaches this

question with hesitation. Rao states that the Internet does free

people from their geography, connecting a multitude of perspectives

from around the world, and it does provide a means of securing

information twenty-four hours a day, but Rao thinks the

psychological price tag for these services may be higher than we

imagined. Cyberfriends can be made easily, perhaps too easily.

''[T]he ease with which they form these links means that many are

likely to be trivial, shortlived, and disposable—junk friends. We may

be overwhelmed by a continuous static of information and casual

acquaintance, so that finding true soul mates will be even harder

than it is today'' (Rao 98). In an age where relationships are

unstable, divorce is rampant, and children are abandoned or

Short quotation: Brackets establish quote as a complete sentence.

Vickery 7

neglected, the ''if I don't like it I can change rooms or sign off''
attitude provided by the Internet may be damaging.

Yet many would disagree. Talk shows parade in front of the
cameras a multitude of happy couples who met over the Internet.
Since their physical identities were hidden, they judged one another
by their conversations before falling in love. These couples believe
that their love is more ''genuine'' because it developed from
content (opinions and feelings) as opposed to package (physical
looks). Only time will tell if their predictions are correct.

Other Internet users do not really care about the stability of
their online relationships. What matters most to them is the
opportunity for conversation, no matter what the content of those
conversations may be. David Boylan, an at-home father raising two
young children, often visits ''Parent Soup,'' an ad-supported online
community. Boylan states, ''In my nine years as a stay-at-home
dad, I spent a lot of time saying gah-gah, goo-goo and dying for
some intellectual stimulation. The camaraderie is so cool—you can't
get that from a magazine'' (qtd. in Levine 168–69). Boylan doesn't
care if he talks about whooping cough or ticks, as long as he gets to
talk. Several homebound mothers have expressed the same
sentiment.

So the Internet does provide for one of our most basic needs:
companionship. It also gives the people who have access an
enormous sense of freedom. Whether a person is trapped within
his/her home, disabled, or just plain shy, the Internet allows for

Short quotation: quotation *within* source quoted.

Vickery 8

Documentation: Both author and title of source are identified in introductory independent clause.

movements and encounters at a dizzying speed. Sherry Turkle, author of <u>Life on the Screen</u>, examines the implications of this new form of self-expression and self-determination: ''On MUDs, one's body is represented by one's own textual description, so the obese can be slender, the beautiful plain, the 'nerdy' sophisticated'' (12). This freedom, Turkle claims, allows ''new ways of thinking about evolution, relationships, sexuality, politics, and identity'' (26). Males are females, old are young, white are black, and the poor are aristocrats. Since nothing can be taken for granted in cyberspace, our biases and prejudices may be exposed, contemplated, and amended.

Summary: Major points in sections of source are summarized.

Far from being threatening, Turkle believes this experience can be quite liberating. Men who want to experience what women encounter (and vice versa) may do so thanks to virtual crossdressing (gender-swapping). Turkle follows the progress of a thirty-four-year-old male, an industrial designer, who MUDed as a female character. As Mairead, a commoner in a medieval world, he met a nobleman who wanted to marry him (virtually). Mairead said yes and the services were conducted online. After the marriage, however, this male engineer was shocked by the way Mairead's virtual husband treated her:

> But everytime [sic] I behave like I'm now going to be a countess some day, you know, assert myself—as in, ''And I never liked this wallpaper anyway''—I get pushed down. The relationship is pull up, push down. It's an

incredibly psychologically damaging thing to do to a

person. And the very thing that he liked about her—that

she was independent, strong, said what was on her

mind—it is all being bled out of her. (214)

Documentation:

Although sexism is as prevalent on the Internet as it is in real

life, some men are noticing and experiencing it for the first time.

Documentation:
In "block" quotation
period goes *before*
parenthetical
reference. In short
quotations the
period goes *after* the
parenthetical
reference.

The man in Turkle's case study is learning that ''some of the

things that work when you're a man just backfire when you're a

woman'' (214). Although some women pose as males on the

Internet in order to experience what it means to be a man, many

pose as a male simply to avoid these kinds of unpleasant

encounters.

For those who do not want to role play, adopt a different

identity, or get in touch with a different aspect of themselves, the

Internet can still be a means of validation. For example, many

college graduates are optimistic about their future lives. They

imagine a house in the suburbs, a high-paying job, a spouse and

family, and perhaps a two-car garage. Due to the deplorable state of

the job market, however, these graduates find themselves trapped in

low-paying, intellectually unchallenging jobs, living in unsafe

neighborhoods, and isolated from their intellectual peers. Turkle

argues that the Internet helps these people establish a link with

people who will see them as they see themselves: ''MUDs provide

them with the sense of a middle-class peer group. So it is really not

that surprising that it is in virtual social life they feel most like

Documentation:
Author's name is
cited at beginning
of independent
clause; quote
follows colon
(parenthetical
reference follows
quotation).

Vickery 10

themselves'' (240). This type of self-affirmation is called escapism by some, therapy by others. Whether it is a way out, a way back, or a way forward probably depends on the psychological needs of the individual.

The debate continues. The Internet is said to be a haven for social misfits, but it is also lauded as a source of connection and community. Some users find chat groups organized around topics of interest, such as parenting skills, literature, or feature films, while other users find virtual rape and degradation. What is accepted without question is that such groups are here to stay. Furthermore, they are ''growing faster than O.J. Simpson's legal bills'' (Elmer-Dewitt 50). As in real life, individuals online will have to decide how much time and money they want to invest in searching for meaningful conversations.

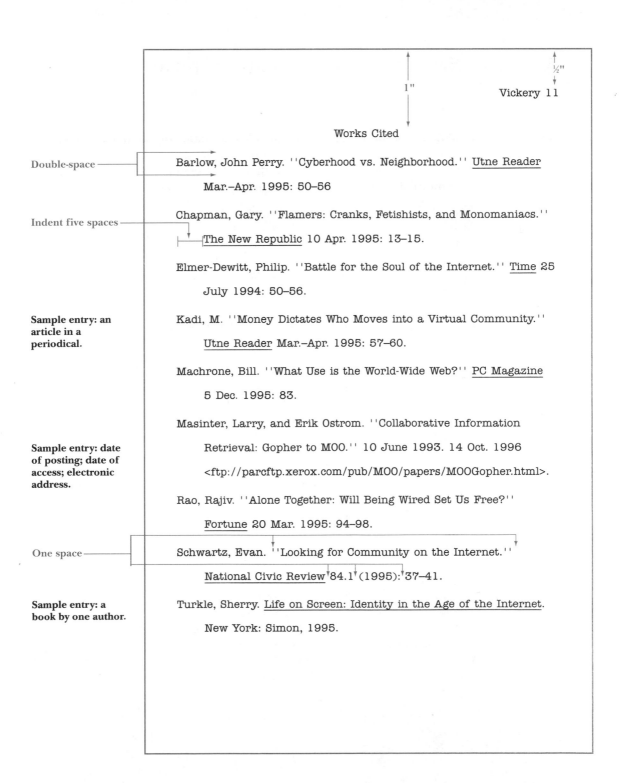

Vickery 11

½"

1"

Works Cited

Double-space

Barlow, John Perry. ''Cyberhood vs. Neighborhood.'' <u>Utne Reader</u> Mar.–Apr. 1995: 50–56

Indent five spaces

Chapman, Gary. ''Flamers: Cranks, Fetishists, and Monomaniacs.'' <u>The New Republic</u> 10 Apr. 1995: 13–15.

Elmer-Dewitt, Philip. ''Battle for the Soul of the Internet.'' <u>Time</u> 25 July 1994: 50–56.

Sample entry: an article in a periodical.

Kadi, M. ''Money Dictates Who Moves into a Virtual Community.'' <u>Utne Reader</u> Mar.–Apr. 1995: 57–60.

Machrone, Bill. ''What Use is the World-Wide Web?'' <u>PC Magazine</u> 5 Dec. 1995: 83.

Masinter, Larry, and Erik Ostrom. ''Collaborative Information Retrieval: Gopher to MOO.'' 10 June 1993. 14 Oct. 1996 <ftp://parcftp.xerox.com/pub/MOO/papers/MOOGopher.html>.

Sample entry: date of posting; date of access; electronic address.

Rao, Rajiv. ''Alone Together: Will Being Wired Set Us Free?'' <u>Fortune</u> 20 Mar. 1995: 94–98.

One space

Schwartz, Evan. ''Looking for Community on the Internet.'' <u>National Civic Review</u> 84.1 (1995): 37–41.

Sample entry: a book by one author.

Turkle, Sherry. <u>Life on Screen: Identity in the Age of the Internet</u>. New York: Simon, 1995.

6. Abbreviations for MLA Documentation

Selected Publishers

When the publisher's name includes the name of one person (Harry N. Abrams, Inc.), cite the surname alone (Abrams). When the publisher's name includes the name of more than one person (Harcourt Brace), cite only the first of these names (Harcourt).

Abrams	Harry N. Abrams, Inc.
Allyn	Allyn and Bacon, Inc.
Appleton	Appleton-Century-Crofts
Basic	Basic Books
Bowker	R. R. Bowker Co.
Dodd	Dodd, Mead, and Co.
Doubleday	Doubleday and Co., Inc.
Farrar	Farrar, Straus, and Giroux, Inc.
Feminist	The Feminist Press at the City University of New York
Harcourt	Harcourt Brace
Harper	HarperCollins
Harvard UP	Harvard University Press
Holt	Holt, Rinehart and Winston, Inc.
Houghton	Houghton Mifflin Co.
Knopf	Alfred A. Knopf, Inc.
Lippincott	J. B. Lippincott Co.
MIT P	The MIT Press
MLA	The Modern Language Association of America
Norton	W. W. Norton and Co., Inc.
Oxford UP	Oxford University Press, Inc.
Princeton UP	Princeton University Press
Rand	Rand McNally and Co.
Random	Random House, Inc.
St. Martin's	St. Martin's Press, Inc.
Scribner's	Charles Scribner's Sons
Simon	Simon and Schuster, Inc.
UMI	University Microfilms International
U of Chicago P	University of Chicago Press
Viking	The Viking Press, Inc.
Yale UP	Yale University Press

Selected Reference Resources

BM	British Museum, London (now British Library)
Cong. Rec.	*Congressional Record*
DA, DAI	*Dissertation Abstracts, Dissertation Abstracts International*
DAB	*Dictionary of American Biography*
DNB	*Dictionary of National Biography*
ERIC—ED	Educational Resources Information Center—Educational Document
ERIC—EJ	Educational Resources Information Center—Educational Journal
GPO	Government Printing Office, Washington D.C.
HMSO	Her (His) Majesty's Stationery Office
LC	Library of Congress
NPR	National Public Radio
PBS	Public Broadcasting System
PC-DOS	Personal Computer-Disk Operating System

Appendix on APA Style

The purpose of documentation is twofold: (1) to avoid representing somebody else's work as your own and (2) to refer readers to the specific source you are citing. Although there is general agreement about the purpose of documentation, different fields of knowledge use different styles. If you are writing a research paper in the humanities, your instructor is likely to require MLA style. If you are writing a research paper in the social sciences, your instructor is likely to require APA (American Psychological Association) style.

In some ways, APA and MLA styles are similar. Both require an alphabetized list of sources and in-text parenthetical documentation of citations. Both use numbered notes only to convey certain kinds of information not included in the text. Some major differences between the two styles, especially APA's emphasis on date of publication, are reflected in the guidelines and illustrations given below. For further information, see the APA *Publication Manual.*[1]

---

[1]American Psychological Association, *Publication Manual of the American Psychological Association,* 4th ed. (Washington: APA, 1994).

Preparing the List of References

1. Paginate the list of sources (entitled **References**) as a continuation of your text.

2. Double-space between successive lines of an entry and between entries.

3. Begin the first line of an entry flush left, and indent successive lines three spaces.

4. List the entries in alphabetical order according to the last name of the author.

5. If you are listing more than one work by the same author, arrange the works by date of publication, starting with the earliest work. Repeat the author's name in each entry.

6. Invert the names of all authors in each entry, and use initials for the first and middle names of all authors.

7. When there is more than one author, use an ampersand (&) before the name of the last author.

8. When there is more than one author, name all the authors in the list of references. (In the text, if there are more than six authors, list only the first author and use *et al.* for the rest.)

9. Place the date of publication in parentheses immediately after the author's name. Place a period after the closing parenthesis.

10. If you list two works by the same author published in the same year, arrange the works alphabetically by title (excluding the articles *a* and *the*), and assign letters to the year to prevent confusion—(1984a), (1984b).

11. Place the article title (if any) or book title after the year of publication.

12. In references to books, capitalize only the first word of the book title, the first word of the book subtitle (if any), and all proper names. Underline the complete book title.

13. If the author is also the publisher of the work, put the word *Author* after the place of publication.

14. In references to articles in periodicals or in edited volumes, capitalize only the first word of the article title, the first word of the article subtitle (if any), and all proper names. Do not enclose the article title in quotation marks. Put a period after the article title.

15. Spell out the names of journals in upper- and lowercase letters, and underline the journal name.

16. In references to periodicals, give the volume number in arabic numerals, and underline it. Do not use *vol.* before the number.

17. Use *p.* or *pp.* for page numbers in references to newspapers and magazines. Omit *p.* or *pp.* in references to journal articles.

Sample Entries

When citing books and articles, provide the following general categories of information:

Author's last name, first initial. (Publication date). <u>Book title</u>. Additional

  information. City of publication: Publishing company.

Author's last name, first initial. (Publication date). Article title. <u>Periodical title</u>,

  inclusive pages.

Entries illustrating variations on this basic format appear below and are numbered to facilitate reference. To compare these entries with those documented in MLA style, refer to the page and item numbers given in brackets.

A Book by One Author

1. Boorstin, D. (1992). <u>The creators: A history of the heroes of the</u>

    <u>imagination</u>. New York: Random House.   [3,1]

Two or More Books by the Same Author

2. Garreau, J. (1981). <u>The nine nations of North America</u>. Boston: Houghton

    Mifflin.   [3,3]

3. Garreau, J. (1991). <u>Edge city: Life on the new frontier</u>. New York:

    Doubleday.   [3,2]

A Book by More Than One Author

4. Belenky, M. F., Clichy, B. M., Goldberger, N. R., & Torule, J. M. (1986). Women's ways of knowing: The development of self, voice, and mind. New York: Basic Books.   [4,6]

A Book by a Corporate Author

5. Boston Women's Health Book Collective. (1973). Our bodies, ourselves: A book by and for women. Boston: Author.   [4,7]

A Work in an Anthology

6. Silko, L. M. (1991). The man to send rain clouds. In W. Brown and A. Ling (Eds.), Imagining America: Stories from the promised land. New York: Persea.   [5,13]

A Signed Article from a Daily Newspaper

7. Barringer, F. (1993, March 7). Where many elderly live, signs of the future. The New York Times, p. 12.   [7,28]

An Article from a Weekly or Biweekly Magazine

8. Trillin, C. (1993, February 15). Culture shopping. The New Yorker, pp. 48–51.   [7,31]

An Article in a Journal with Continuous Pagination

9. Elbow, P. (1993). Ranking, evaluating, and liking: Sorting out three forms of judgment. College English, 55, 187–206.   [8,32]

CD-ROM: Printed Source or Printed Analogue

10. West, Cornel. (1987). The dilemma of the black intellectual. [CD–ROM]. Critical Quarterly, 29, 39–52. From: SilverPlatter File: MLA International Bibliography Item: 8800011.   [9,38]

Documenting Sources

The following guidelines and examples emphasize the major differences between APA and MLA styles of documentation.

1. When you are summarizing or paraphrasing a source and do not mention the author's name in your sentence, place the author's name and date of publication in parentheses. Separate each unit of information with a comma.

   Fairy tales help children explore the worlds of forbidden knowledge

   (Tuan, 1979).

2. When you are quoting and do not mention the author's name in your sentence, place the author's name, date of publication, and page number(s) in parentheses.

   Although fairy tales contain frightening information, they ''thrill

   rather than terrify a healthy child'' (Tuan, 1979, p. 20).

3. When you are quoting and you mention the name of the author in your sentence, place only the publication date and page number(s) in parentheses.

   Tuan (1979) suggests that the effect of fairy tales is muted by

   ''the affectionate environment in which the stories are usually told''

   (p. 20).

4. If you use more than one source written in the same year by the same author, follow the pattern established in your reference list, and include the letter assigned to the source.

   (Turnbull, 1965b)

5. If you cite several sources in one place, list them in alphabetical order by authors' last names, and separate them with a semicolon.

   The Mbuti Pygmies, carefree and harmonious, have no concept of evil

   and thus no real sense of fear (Tuan, 1979; Turnbull, 1965a).

References

Tuan, Y. (1979). Landscapes of fear. New York: Pantheon.

Turnbull, C. M. (1965a). The Mbuti Pygmies of the Congo. In J. L. Gibbs, Jr. (Ed.), Peoples of Africa (pp. 281–317). New York: Holt, Rinehart and Winston.

Turnbull, C. M. (1965b). Wayward servants: The two worlds of the African Pygmies. Garden City, NY: Natural History Press.

Index

abbreviations
    of publishers, 40
    of reference resources, 41
    in Works Cited, 2, 40–41
abstracts, in Works Cited, 8
addresses, in Works Cited, 13
advertisements, in Works Cited, 13
afterwords, in Works Cited, 5
alphabetization
    of anonymous works, 18
    of authors with same last name, 16
    of multiple books by same author, 2
anonymous works
    articles
        in newspapers, 7
        in parenthetical reference, 18
        in reference books, 6
        in Works Cited, 6
    books
        in parenthetical reference, 18
        in Works Cited, 4, 6, 18
anthologies, in Works Cited, 4–5
APA (American Psychological Association) documentation style, 41–46
    documentation, 45–46
    References, 42–44, 46
arabic numerals
    in parenthetical reference, 19
    in Works Cited, 2
articles on Internet, 11
articles, one-page, in parenthetical reference, 18
    see also Works Cited
artworks, in Works Cited, 12
authors
    anonymous
        in parenthetical reference, 18
        in Works Cited, 4, 18

corporate
    in parenthetical reference, 18–19
    in Works Cited, 4
multiple
    in parenthetical reference, 17
    in Works Cited, 3–4
single, in parenthetical reference, 14
single, in Works Cited
    multiple books by, 3
    one book by, 3
with same last name, 16–17

Bibliography, 1
    see also References; Works Cited
books
    authors of
        anonymous, 4
        corporate, 4
        multiple, 2, 3–4
        single, 2, 3
    editors of, 4
    on Internet, 10
    published before 1900, 6
    republished, 5
    series, 5
    titles of, 2
        within titles, 6
    translations, 6
    see also Works Cited

cartoons, in Works Cited, 13
CD-ROMs
    medium
        work in more than one, 9
    nonperiodical publication, 9
    periodical publication, 9
    printed source or printed analogue, 9
    in Works Cited, 9
charts, in Works Cited, 13
classic works, in parenthetical reference, 19

colon
    for quotations, 23
    in Works Cited, 2–3
        with books, 3
        with periodicals, 7
comma, with parenthetical reference, 15–16
compilations, in Works Cited, 4
corporate authors, see authors

database, articles on, 11
discussion group, posting on Internet, 11
Dissertation Abstracts, in Works Cited, 8
Dissertation Abstracts International, in Works Cited, 8
dissertations, see Works Cited

editions, in Works Cited, 5
editorials, in Works Cited, 8
editors, in Works Cited, 4
electronic sources, in Works Cited, 9–11
ellipsis, for quotations, 22
e-mail message, 11–12
endnotes, 1, 21
    see also notes
et al., in parenthetical reference, 17

films, in Works Cited, 2, 12
footnotes, 1, 21
    see also notes
forewords, in Works Cited, 5

government documents
    in parenthetical reference, 18–19
    in Works Cited, 6

headings, of research paper, 27
hyphens, in author position in Works Cited, 2, 3

imprints of publishers, in
     Works Cited, 4
indentation
     for quotations, 23–24
     in Works Cited, 2
Internet and World Wide Web
     articles published on
          in journal, 11
          in magazine, 11
          in reference database, 11
     database on, 11
     e-mail message, 11–12
     MLA Web site on, 10
     personal Web site on, 10
     poem published on, 10
     posting to discussion group,
          11
     professional Web site on, 10
     review published on, 11
     speed of change on, 10
     in Works Cited, 9–11
interviews, in Works Cited, 13
in-text references, 14, 15, 16,
     17, 18, 19
introductions, in Works Cited,
     5
italics, with titles, 2

journals, in Works Cited, 8

lectures, in Works Cited, 2, 12
letters, in Works Cited, 13
list of works cited, *see* Works
     Cited
literary works, in parentheti-
     cal reference, 19

magazines, in Works Cited, 7
maps, in Works Cited, 13
medium
     work in more than one, 9
MLA (Modern Language As-
     sociation)
     documentation style of, 1
     Web site of, 10
multiple authors, *see* authors
multiple works
     by multiple authors in par-
          enthetical reference,
          19–20
     by same author
          in parenthetical refer-
               ence, 16

     in Works Cited, 2
multivolume works
     in parenthetical reference,
          17
     in Works Cited, 5

newspapers, in Works Cited, 7
nonperiodical publication, 9
note cards, 22
     see also note taking
notes, 1, 20–21
     additional commentary on
          information in text sup-
          plied by, 20
     additional sources listed in,
          20–21
     endnotes, 1, 21
     footnotes, 1, 21
     form, 20–21
     placement, 21
     sources listed in, 21
     Works Cited and, 21
note taking
     note cards for, 22
     paraphrasing, 24–25
     plagiarism and, 22, 23,
          25–26
     quoting, 22–24
     summarizing, 24–25
novels, in parenthetical refer-
     ence, 19
numerals, superscript, 21
     see also arabic numerals; ro-
          man numerals

omissions from quotations,
     22
outline, sample, 27–28

pagination
     of journal articles
          with continuous pagina-
               tion, 8
          with separate pagination,
               8
     of research paper, 27
     of Works Cited, 1
pamphlets, in Works Cited, 2
paraphrasing, for note taking,
     24–25
parenthetical references,
     14–21
     to anonymous works, 18

     in APA style, 45
     arabic numerals in, 19
     authors in, 14
          corporate, 18–19
          having same last name as
               another in Works
               Cited, 16–17
          multiple, 17–18
          of two or more works, 16
     to classic works, 19
     to entire work, 14
     to government documents,
          18–19
     guidelines for, 14–16
     in-text references and, 14,
          15, 17, 18, 19
     to literary works, 19
     multiple works in single ref-
          erence, 19–20
     to multivolume works, 17
     to one-page article, 18
     to one work by author of
          two or more works,
          16–17
     placement of, 15–16
     punctuation of, 15–16,
          19–20
     to quotations, 15, 23
     roman numerals in, 19
     by title, 16
     uses of, 20–21
     to work by multiple au-
          thors, 17
     Works Cited and, 14, 16, 17,
          18, 19, 20
performances, in Works Cited,
     12
period
     for ellipsis, 22
     with quotations, 23
     in Works Cited, 2
periodicals, *see* Works Cited
personal Web site, 10
placement
     of parenthetical reference,
          15–16
     of Works Cited, 1
plagiarism, avoiding, 22, 24,
     25–26
plays
     in parenthetical reference,
          19

in Works Cited, 2
poems
  on Internet, 10
  in parenthetical reference, 19
  in Works Cited, 2, 10
prefaces, in Works Cited, 5
printed source or printed analogue, 9
proceedings, in Works Cited, 6
professional Web site, 10
publishers
  abbreviations of, 40
  in Works Cited, 2, 40
    imprints, 4
punctuation
  in parenthetical reference, 15–16, 19
  in Works Cited, 2
  see also individual punctuation marks (e.g., comma; period)

quotation marks
  with quotations, 22–24
  with titles, 2
    with quotations in, 8
quotations
  ellipsis for, 22
  introduced with sentence and colon, 23–24
  long, 15, 23–24
    summary of, 24
  in note taking, 22–23
  paraphrasing, 24–25
  parenthetical reference to, 15, 23–24
  set off with introductory sentence followed by colon, 23
  into syntax of your sentence, 23
  in titles, 8

radio programs, in Works Cited, 12
recordings, in Works Cited, 12
reference books, articles from, in Works Cited, 5–6
reference database, 11
reference resources, abbreviations of, 41

references, APA, 42–44, 46
republished books, in Works Cited, 5
research paper
  headings in, 27
  outline for, 27–28
  page numbers in, 27
  sample, 28–39
  spacing in, 27, 29
  title of, 27, 28, 29
reviews, in Works Cited, 8, 11
roman numerals
  in parenthetical reference, 19
  in Works Cited, 2

sample entries
  for References (APA), 43–44
  for Works Cited
    articles, 5, 6, 7–8
    books, 3–7
    CD-ROMs, 9
    Internet and World Wide Web sources, 9–11
    other sources, 10–11
semicolon, in parenthetical reference, 19
series, in Works Cited, 5
short stories, in Works Cited, 2
social sciences, APA documentation for, 41–46
song titles, in Works Cited, 2
source cards, 21–23
spacing
  of ellipsis points, 22
  of research paper, 27, 28
  of Works Cited, 2
speeches, in Works Cited, 2, 13
summarizing, 24
superscript numeral, 21

television programs, in Works Cited, 12
title page, of research paper, 27
titles
  alphabetization of, 18
  italics for, 2
  parenthetical reference using, 18
  punctuation of, 2, 3
  quotation marks with, 2

quotations in, 8
  of research paper, 27, 28, 29
  shortened, 16
  within titles
    of articles in Works Cited, 8
    of books in Works Cited, 2, 6
translations, in Works Cited, 6

underlining, *see* italics
unpublished works, *see* Works Cited

Web sites, 9–10
Works Cited, 1–13
  abbreviations in, 2, 7
  abstracts in, 8
  addresses in, 13
  advertisements in, 13
  afterwords in, 5
  anthologies in, 4–5
  arrangement of, 2
    by title, 18
  articles in, 5–8, 11
    anonymous, 6
    on Internet, 11
    journal, 8
    magazine, 7
    newspapers, 7
    reference book, 5–6
  artworks in, 12
  books in, 2, 3–7, 10
    published before 1900, 6
    published on Internet, 10
    series, 5
    titles of, 2
    titles within titles of, 6
    translations, 6
  cartoons in, 13
  CD-ROM
    medium
      work in more than one, 9
    nonperiodical publication, 9
    periodical publication, 9
    printed source or printed analogue, 9
  charts in, 13
  compilations in, 4
  discussion group in, 11

dissertation abstracts in, 8
dissertations in, 2
  published, 7
  unpublished, 6
editions in, 5
editorials in, 8
editors in, 4
electronic sources in, 9–11
e-mail messages in, 11–12
films in, 2, 12
forewords in, 5
government documents in, 6
information services in, 9
interviews in, 13
in-text references and, 14
Internet and World Wide Web sources in, 9–11
introductions in, 5
journals in, 8
lectures in, 2, 13
letters in, 13
magazines in, 7
maps in, 13
multivolume works in, 5

newspapers in, 7
notes and, 21
numerals in, 2
pamphlets in, 2
parenthetical references and, 14, 16, 17, 18, 19, 20
performances in, 12
periodicals in, 2, 7–8, *see also* articles in, *herein*
  with continuous pagination, 8
  with separate pagination, 8
placement of, 1
plays in, 2
poems in, 2, 10
posting to discussion group in, 11
prefaces in, 5
preparation of, 21–22
proceedings in, 6
provisional list of, 22
publication information in, 2

publishers in, 2, 40
  imprints, 4
punctuation in, 2
radio programs in, 12
recordings in, 12
republished books in, 5
reviews in, 8, 11
short stories in, 2
source cards and, 21–22
spacing of, 2
speeches in, 2, 13
television programs in, 12
translations in, 6
unpublished works in, 2
  dissertations, 6
  letters, 13
  works of art in, 12
  Web sites in, 10
see also References, APA
Works Consulted, 1
see also Works Cited
World Wide Web, *see* Internet and World Wide Web